W9-DDC-682

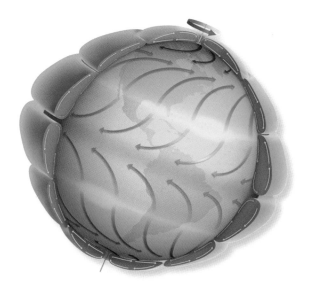

Published in 2014 by The Rosen Publishing Group, Inc.
29 East 21st Street, New York, NY 10010

Photo Credits: **KEY** tl=top left; tc=top center; tr=top right; cl=center left; c=center; cr=center right; bl=bottom left; br=bottom right; bg=background

DSCD = Digitalstock; iS = istockphoto.com; MAY = Mayang.com; N_MI = NASA Missions; SH = Shutterstock; TPL = photolibrary.com

front cover bl iS; **8**tr iS; bl, br DSCD; **9**tl, tr iS; bl, br DSCD; **14-15**c iS; **16**cl iS; **17**bl, br, cl, cr, tr MAY; br, cl, cr, tr SH; bl TPL; **18**cl iS; bl DSCD; **19**cr iS; **24-25**bg iS; **26**cl N_MI; **27**tc MAY; **29**cr GI; **30**br, c, cr SH

All illustrations copyright Weldon Owen Pty Ltd

Weldon Owen Pty Ltd
Managing Director: Kay Scarlett
Creative Director: Sue Burk
Publisher: Helen Bateman
Senior Vice President, International Sales: Stuart Laurence
Vice President Sales North America: Ellen Towell
Administration Manager, International Sales: Kristine Ravn

Publisher Cataloging Data

Close, Edward.
All about the weather / by Edward Close.
p. cm. — (Discovery education: earth and space science)
Includes index.
ISBN 978-1-4777-6190-8 (library binding) — ISBN 978-1-4777-6192-2 (pbk.) —
ISBN 978-1-4777-6193-9 (6-pack)
1. Weather — Juvenile literature. 2. Meteorology — Juvenile literature. I. Close, Edward. II. Title.
QC981.3 C55 2014
551.5—d23

Manufactured in the United States of America

CPSIA Compliance Information: Batch #W14PK2: For Further Information contact Rosen Publishing, New York, New York at 1-800-237-9932

EARTH AND SPACE SCIENCE

ALL ABOUT THE WEATHER

EDWARD CLOSE

PowerKiDS press.

New York

Contents

The Sun's Power

Ocean storm

All weather on Earth is fueled by the Sun's power. The Sun gives off solar radiation that drives the climate and weather. Its energy warms Earth and allows life to exist. Weather conditions can influence the way people, animals, and plants live. Elements that make up the weather include winds, clouds, storms, rain, and snow. The long-term weather conditions of an area make up its climate.

Heat from the Sun

The Sun's rays deliver a certain amount of energy to Earth. As Earth is a sphere, tropical places near the equator receive the Sun's heat most directly. Near the North and South poles, the Sun is much lower in the sky. These areas are much colder as the Sun's rays are more spread out.

Hurricane

That's Amazing!

Earth is covered by a thin layer of gases called the atmosphere. This wraps around Earth's surface like an orange peel. The atmosphere reaches over 60 miles (100 km) above Earth.

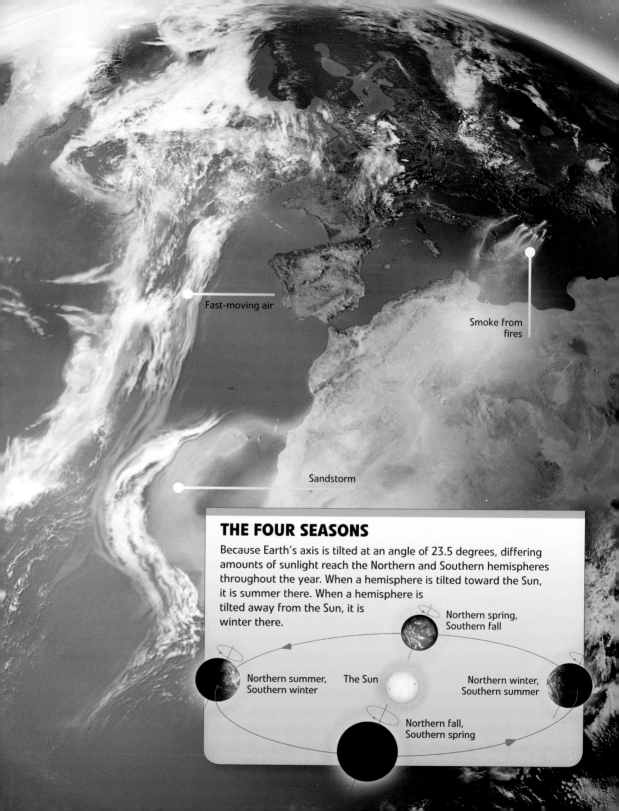

Fast-moving air

Smoke from fires

Sandstorm

THE FOUR SEASONS

Because Earth's axis is tilted at an angle of 23.5 degrees, differing amounts of sunlight reach the Northern and Southern hemispheres throughout the year. When a hemisphere is tilted toward the Sun, it is summer there. When a hemisphere is tilted away from the Sun, it is winter there.

Northern spring,
Southern fall

Northern summer,
Southern winter

The Sun

Northern winter,
Southern summer

Northern fall,
Southern spring

What Is Weather?

Weather is the condition of Earth's atmosphere above us. It can vary from place to place and from day to day. The weather influences where we live, what activities we can do, and even what clothes we wear. Extreme weather can bring fierce blizzards and storms, long droughts, heat waves, and wildfires.

Rain

Rain is vital to life. In places where rain is scarce, there are few people, plants, or animals. Crops need rain to grow, and animals need water to survive.

Snow

In very cold weather, snow may blanket the ground. Blizzards may cause roads to be closed, planes to be grounded, and trains halted.

Flood

A flood occurs when heavy rain falls, the soil can no longer absorb the rain, and rivers burst their banks. A flood can submerge vast areas of land.

Drought

When there is very little rain in a region for months or even years, a drought may occur. Crops will die, rivers will dry up, and livestock will suffer.

Hurricane

A hurricane is a large tropical storm with extremely powerful winds. This huge storm brings heavy rain and can often destroy buildings and trees.

Lightning

During powerful thunderstorms, lightning strikes can occur. Lightning forms from a buildup of electrical energy within a thunderstorm cloud.

Tornado

A tornado is a small, but fierce rotating column of air that reaches from the clouds to the ground. Tornadoes commonly occur in a region known as Tornado Alley in the US.

Whirling Winds

Wind is air in motion through the atmosphere. Wind carries warm and cold air around the globe. Sometimes winds can be very gentle. At other times the wind is extremely powerful, blowing down trees and destroying buildings.

Air pressure
A high-pressure system indicates that the air is packed more tightly, or is more dense. Low-pressure air is less dense. High pressure usually produces fine weather, while low pressure usually brings stormy weather.

Trade winds
Easterly winds blow toward the equator.

Rising air
In a low-pressure system, warm surface air spirals upward. Rising moisture cools and condenses, forming clouds and often rain.

Sinking air
As air spirals downward, high pressure forms at the surface. The air warms, which causes precipitation to evaporate and clouds to break up.

Winds
As winds blow from high pressure to low pressure, a closed circulation system develops.

Westerlies
Warm, gusty winds blow from the west in the midlatitudes.

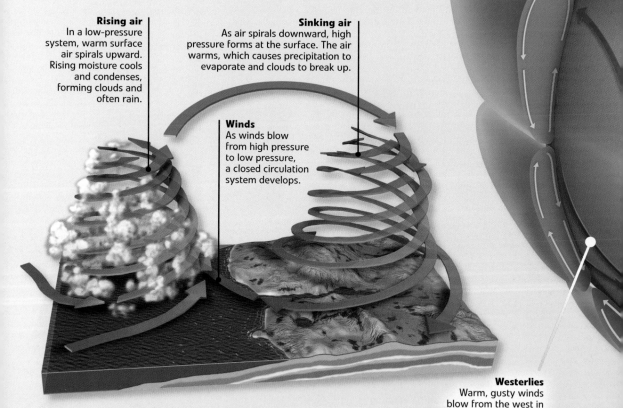

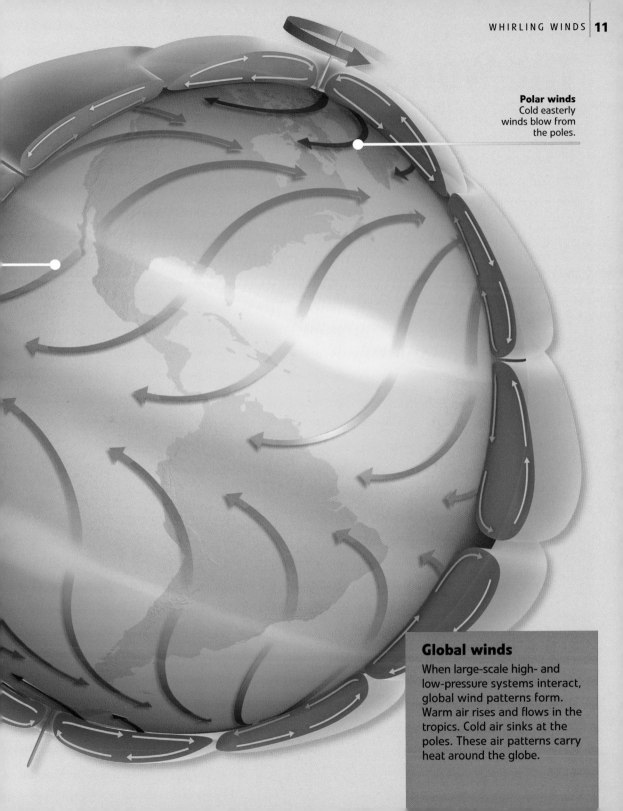

Polar winds
Cold easterly winds blow from the poles.

Global winds

When large-scale high- and low-pressure systems interact, global wind patterns form. Warm air rises and flows in the tropics. Cold air sinks at the poles. These air patterns carry heat around the globe.

The World's Water

All life on Earth needs water to survive. More than 97 percent of this water is in liquid form in the oceans that cover 71 percent of Earth's surface. The Sun powers the never-ending process known as the water cycle that circulates the water between the land, oceans, and air.

The water cycle

When the Sun's rays heat the surface of the oceans, lakes, and rivers, the water evaporates and turns into water vapor. The water vapor combines to form clouds in the sky. These clouds produce rain or snow, which falls back to Earth.

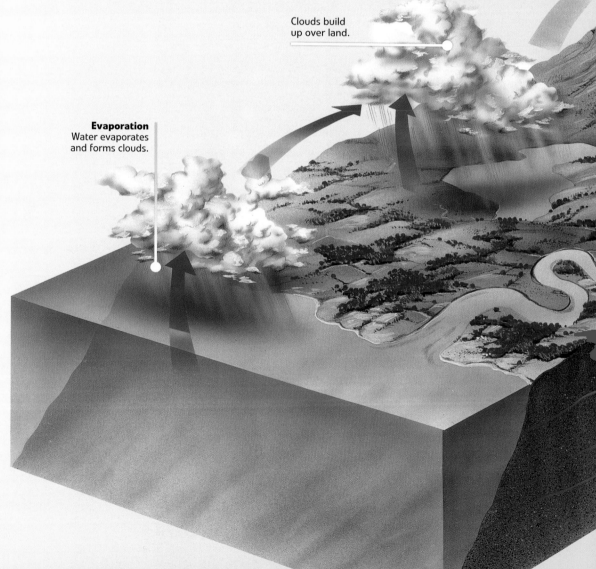

Clouds build up over land.

Evaporation
Water evaporates and forms clouds.

Rain falls from clouds.

That's Amazing!

Although Earth has vast amounts of water, very little is drinkable. Only 3 percent of Earth's water is fresh water and most of this exists as ice.

Water droplets
Millions of water droplets are needed to make one drop of rain. If the raindrops grow large enough, they will fall to Earth.

Drainage
Rainwater drains into lakes, rivers, and underground channels.

Back to the ocean
Water flows back to the sea via rivers and underground channels.

Frozen water
In freezing cold air, water vapor changes to ice or snow. The air temperature, water vapor, and ice crystals in a cloud determine the shape of a snowflake.

Waves in Motion

Waves occur when an outside force creates movement of seawater. Most waves are produced by the wind. The wind transfers some of its energy to the ocean surface through friction between the air and water molecules. A tsunami is a huge wave that is not caused by the weather. It can occur when underwater earthquakes, volcanic eruptions, or landslides shake the ocean floor.

Monster waves
Often when there is a large storm, violent winds will create giant ocean waves. These waves tower above the ocean surface, sometimes as high as a five-story building. The enormous force of the wave can destroy boats, beaches, and buildings.

Break point
Closer to shore, the base of the wave slows and the crest breaks over it.

Crest

Trough

Hitting the brakes
Waves slow down as they reach the shore because friction with the shallow ocean floor acts like a brake.

Making waves
Wind blows across the ocean
surface, providing the force
to make waves. A wave
curves up to a narrow
crest, then curves down
to a hollow, called a trough.
The height of the wave
is the distance between
the crest and the trough.

That's Amazing!
A giant ocean wave can travel
faster than 500 miles (800 km) per
hour across the ocean and reach
a height of 100 feet (30 m)
before hitting the shore.

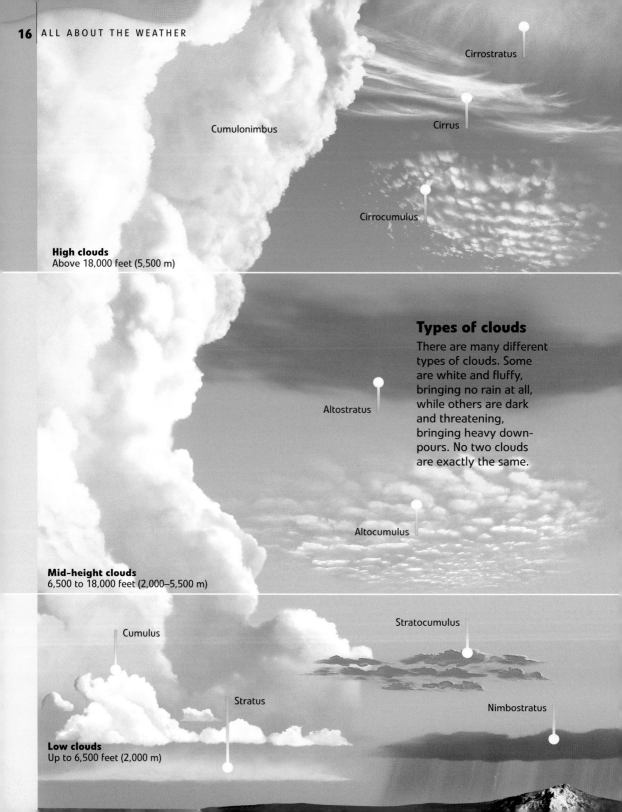

Cirrostratus

Cirrus

Cumulonimbus

Cirrocumulus

High clouds
Above 18,000 feet (5,500 m)

Altostratus

Types of clouds

There are many different types of clouds. Some are white and fluffy, bringing no rain at all, while others are dark and threatening, bringing heavy down-pours. No two clouds are exactly the same.

Altocumulus

Mid-height clouds
6,500 to 18,000 feet (2,000–5,500 m)

Stratocumulus

Cumulus

Stratus

Nimbostratus

Low clouds
Up to 6,500 feet (2,000 m)

Classifying Clouds

Acloud is a large, dense mass of water droplets or ice crystals. Clouds form when warm, moist air rises, expands, and begins to cool. As the air cools, the water vapor it holds condenses into water droplets to form clouds.

Shelf cloud
This is a low-lying, horizontal cloud. Shelf clouds are often described as wedge-shaped, and are attached to the base of a parent cloud.

Cumulus cloud
This is a white, puffy cloud that often appears on sunny days. Sometimes these clouds combine to produce rain, or cumulonimbus, clouds. Cumulus clouds usually form when small pockets of warm air rise.

Funnel cloud
This is a funnel-shaped column of rotating air that comes down from a cumulonimbus cloud, but, unlike a tornado, does not reach the ground. Funnel clouds appear like a cone from the parent cloud.

Lenticular cloud
This is a lens-shaped cloud that is formed by waves of winds high above mountain ranges. Lenticular clouds appear as circular disks hovering at high altitude.

Cumulonimbus cloud
This is a tall, dense thundercloud that towers into the sky. Cumulonimbus clouds are usually associated with wild weather, and often bring rain, hail, and lightning.

Stormy Weather

At times the weather can be extremely violent and severe. Thunderstorms occur when warm, moist air is forced upward by flows or masses of cold air. Large, black thunderclouds stretch miles (km) into the atmosphere, bringing heavy rain and powerful winds.

Upper-level winds

Supercells

As warm air rises, the air inside the cloud rotates because of changes in wind direction. Soon the entire cloud is spinning rapidly. Supercells can produce fierce winds and tornadoes, as well as lightning, hail, and heavy rain.

Hurricanes

Hurricanes start off as tropical storms over the moist, warm waters of the Atlantic and Pacific Oceans. The center of a hurricane is known as the "eye," where there is very little wind. These violent storms bring torrential rain and powerful winds.

Mid-level winds

Tornadoes

Tornadoes are smaller but generally more violent than hurricanes. They consist of funnels of wind that rotate at speeds of up to 280 miles per hour (450 km/h). When a tornado reaches the ground, it can lift up cars, trucks, and even buildings.

Rear flank downdraft

Tracking storms

Storm chasers often track violent storms with special equipment and protected vehicles.

Overshooting top
Powerful updrafts push the cloud above the troposphere.

Updraft
A mesocyclone is a strong rotating updraft.

Lightning strikes
Lightning can burn at temperatures five times hotter than the Sun. A bolt of lightning can be up to 5 miles (8 km) long but is only about as thick as your finger.

Heavy rain or hail

Lethal Lightning

Lightning is an electric current caused by the interaction of positive and negative electric charges inside an enormous thundercloud. Lightning can reach temperatures of 54,000°F (30,000°C). Scientists estimate that 3 million lightning flashes occur daily around the world. Thunder is the sound made by lightning.

Did You Know?

Lightning usually strikes the highest point, such as tall buildings or a tall tree. The Empire State Building in New York City is struck by lightning approximately 100 times each year.

BRANCHING OUT

Lightning can occur when negative charges develop near the base of a cumulonimbus cloud as positive charges are raised by upward drafts. The ground below the thunderstorm becomes positively charged.

Cloud-to-air
Lightning may travel between positive charges inside the cloud to surrounding negatively charged air.

Cloud-to-cloud
Lightning can jump within one cloud or between opposite charges in nearby clouds.

Cloud-to-ground
If there is a positive charge on the ground, lightning may strike downward from the cloud.

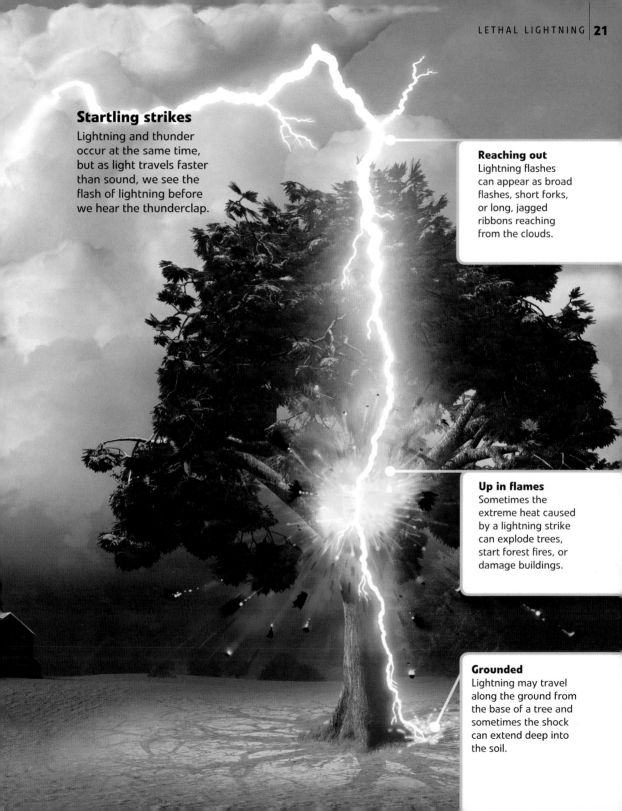

Startling strikes

Lightning and thunder occur at the same time, but as light travels faster than sound, we see the flash of lightning before we hear the thunderclap.

Reaching out

Lightning flashes can appear as broad flashes, short forks, or long, jagged ribbons reaching from the clouds.

Up in flames

Sometimes the extreme heat caused by a lightning strike can explode trees, start forest fires, or damage buildings.

Grounded

Lightning may travel along the ground from the base of a tree and sometimes the shock can extend deep into the soil.

Seek shelter indoors
The best place to seek shelter is in the safety of your home. You can avoid getting into danger by staying indoors until the blizzard passes.

Blustery Blizzards

Blizzards are severe winter storms that produce powerful winds and heavy snow, and possibly sleet or hail. They are a combination of blowing snow and winds of at least 35 miles (56 km) per hour. Visibility can reach near zero, making driving a vehicle on snow-covered roads extremely dangerous.

Snowed under
Sudden heavy dumps of snow can cover cars and houses, making it difficult for people to continue their everyday lives.

In March 1888, a blizzard known as The Great White Hurricane hit New York, killing at least 400 people.

Spectacular snowflakes

Each individual snowflake has its own spectacular, unique shape. The temperature at which ice forms on a tiny piece of dust partly affects the shape of the snowflake.

Help is on its way

If you are ever stuck in a blizzard, stay calm, conserve energy, and wait for help to arrive. Snowmobiles are an ideal rescue vehicle in a blizzard.

AVALANCHE!

An avalanche is a large mass of snow and ice that slides down the slope of a mountain. Large avalanches can bury everything in their path, including trees, cars, houses, and people.

Slippery when wet
Fresh snow falls on top of old snow that is wet or icy.

On the slide
Snow cannot support its own weight and begins to slide down the mountain.

Wave of danger
Sniffer dogs can track down people buried alive in avalanches.

Disastrous Droughts

A drought refers to an extended period, sometimes many years, of very little rainfall in a particular region. Droughts can last for months and sometimes even years. A drought means that farmers will not have enough water in the soil for crops to grow normally or for pastures to produce enough grass for livestock. Without rain, rivers and lakes can dry up and perhaps disappear completely.

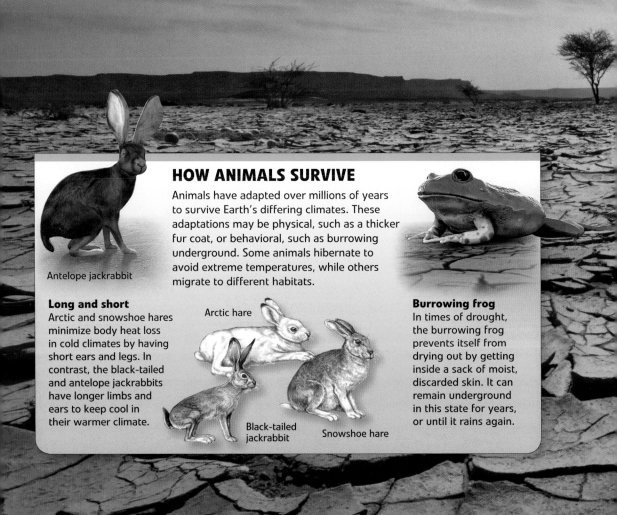

Antelope jackrabbit

HOW ANIMALS SURVIVE

Animals have adapted over millions of years to survive Earth's differing climates. These adaptations may be physical, such as a thicker fur coat, or behavioral, such as burrowing underground. Some animals hibernate to avoid extreme temperatures, while others migrate to different habitats.

Long and short
Arctic and snowshoe hares minimize body heat loss in cold climates by having short ears and legs. In contrast, the black-tailed and antelope jackrabbits have longer limbs and ears to keep cool in their warmer climate.

Arctic hare

Black-tailed jackrabbit

Snowshoe hare

Burrowing frog
In times of drought, the burrowing frog prevents itself from drying out by getting inside a sack of moist, discarded skin. It can remain underground in this state for years, or until it rains again.

Cracked earth

Soil that is starved of water hardens in the sun and shrinks. Then, when it does rain, the ground may be too hard to absorb the water, so it just runs off.

Weather Forecasting

We regularly see weather reports on television, hear them on the radio, or read them on the Internet. But where does this report come from and how do we forecast the weather? Meteorologists are responsible for forecasting weather. They study data and analyze weather patterns to predict what the weather will be like in the days ahead.

Geostationary satellite

Super satellite images
A 3-D satellite image shows Cyclone Favio passing Madagascar in February 2007. The highest clouds of this powerful storm can be seen, colored in red. The use of supercomputers has allowed meteorologists to provide far more accurate weather forecasts.

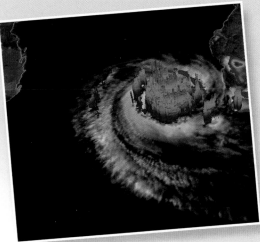

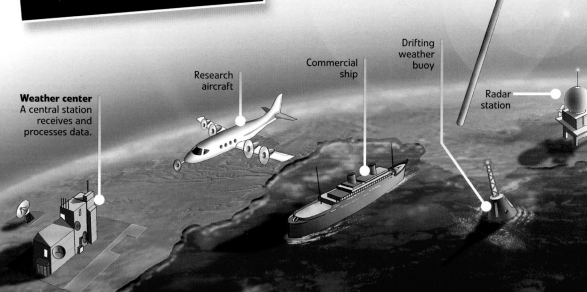

Polar-orbiting satellite

Drifting weather buoy

Commercial ship

Research aircraft

Radar station

Weather center
A central station receives and processes data.

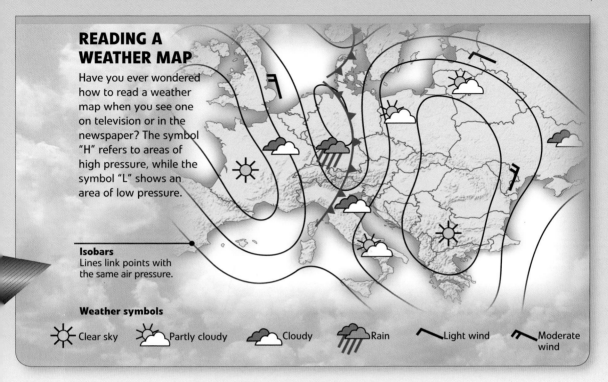

READING A WEATHER MAP

Have you ever wondered how to read a weather map when you see one on television or in the newspaper? The symbol "H" refers to areas of high pressure, while the symbol "L" shows an area of low pressure.

Isobars
Lines link points with the same air pressure.

Weather symbols

Clear sky — Partly cloudy — Cloudy — Rain — Light wind — Moderate wind

Reporting cycle

Many devices are used to collect information and send it through to the weather center. Meteorologists then process this data and produce a weather report. This can then be transmitted around the globe for people to use.

Satellite receivers

Radiosonde balloon

Weather station
Observers staff a manual station.

Oil rig

Commercial airliner

A Changing Climate

Most scientists now agree that Earth is getting warmer. This is having many effects on the environment. The steady rise in Earth's average temperature is known as global warming. There is strong evidence that humans are contributing to this problem. Many scientists have suggested that the rise in temperature will lead to more extreme weather around the globe.

Rising sea levels

As global warming causes temperatures on Earth to rise, ice melts in the polar regions. Ice shelves in the Antarctic are estimated to have been shrinking by 7 percent per decade since the 1950s. This melting ice contributes to rising sea levels. In the last 100 years, sea levels have risen by 8 inches (20 cm). Rising sea levels will cause flooding in many low-lying areas and some small islands will eventually disappear.

ENDANGERED WILDLIFE

Climate change is endangering more animal species—in almost all animal groups—each year. The changing climate and extreme weather are destroying the habitats of many animals, and more are struggling to survive.

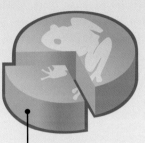

Amphibians
30 percent of species are endangered.

Mammals
22 percent of species are endangered.

Birds
12 percent of species are endangered.

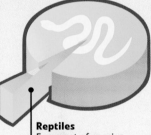

Reptiles
5 percent of species are endangered.

Make Your Own Cloud

Here is an experiment you can try for yourself. Make sure you have adult supervision when making your cloud.

What you need:

☑ One empty, large plastic bottle with a screw-on cap

☑ Warm water

☑ Match

1 Remove the label from the bottle and rinse it well. Do not use soap. Do not dry the inside.

2 Pour a small amount of warm water into the bottle, just to cover the bottom. Screw on the cap and shake it so that water droplets are sticking to the inside. Pour out excess water.

3 Ask a parent to carefully light the match and let it burn to the count of five.

4 Blow out the match and drop it into the bottle.

5 Screw the lid onto the bottle as tightly as you can and shake it two or three times.

6 Slowly squeeze the center of the bottle in and out until a cloud begins to form. This may take a moment or two. You MUST keep squeezing to keep the cloud formed.

7 After several squeezes you should see a cloud that appears when you release your hands. If you do not see a cloud, try placing the bottle near a dark background for contrast.

8 When you are ready to end the experiment, open the bottle and let your cloud escape.

Glossary

adapted (uh-DAPT-ed)
Describes animals that have changed themselves or their behavior in order to survive.

altitude (AL-tuh-tood)
The height of something above ground level or sea level.

atmosphere
(AT-muh-sfeer)
A thin layer of gases surrounding Earth that is retained by Earth's gravity.

axis (AK-sus)
An invisible straight line through Earth's North and South poles around which it rotates.

climate (KLY-mut)
The pattern of weather that occurs in an area over a long period of time.

drought (DROWT)
An extended period of less than average rainfall.

endangered
(in-DAYN-jerd)
Describes a species population that is so small it is in danger of becoming extinct.

evaporate
(ih-VA-puh-rayt)
To turn liquid into a vapor state.

forecasting
(FOR-kas-ting)
The use of technology and science by meteorologists to predict what the weather will be like in a certain place in the future.

friction
(FRIK-shin)
The resistance produced when one object rubs against another.

global warming
(GLOH-bul WOR-ming)
An increase in the average temperature of Earth's atmosphere.

humidity
(hyoo-MIH-duh-tee)
The amount of moisture in the air.

ice crystals (YS KRIS-tulz)
Small particles of ice which bind together to form clouds, frost, and ice fog.

meteorologist
(mee-tee-uh-RAH-luh-jist)
A scientist who studies processes in Earth's atmosphere that cause weather conditions.

radiation
(ray-dee-AY-shun)
The Sun's energy that is radiated or transmitted in the form of rays or waves.

satellites (SA-tih-lyts)
Spacecraft that orbit around Earth and observe the atmosphere and the weather.

snowmobile
(SNOH-moh-beel)
A vehicle with tracks designed for travel on snow using skis on its front.

supercells
(SOO-per-selz)
Large thunderstorms that are characterized by the presence of a deep, rotating updraft.

troposphere
(TROH-puh-sfeer)
The lowest layer of Earth's atmosphere. It is up to 12 miles (20 km) thick.

tsunami (soo-NAH-mee)
A large sea wave produced by an earthquake or volcanic eruption under the sea.

updraft (UP-draft)
A current of air that blows upward.

weather (Weh-thur)
A current of air that blows upward.

Index

A
air pressure 10, 27
Antarctic 28
Arctic 24
atmosphere 6, 8, 10, 18
avalanche 23
axis 7

B
blizzard 8, 22, 23

C
cloud 6, 9, 10, 12, 13, 16, 17,
    18, 19, 20, 21, 30
cumulonimbus 16, 17, 20

D
drought 8, 9, 24

E
earthquake 14
endangered animals 29
equator 6, 10

F
flood 8, 28
forecasting 26, 27

friction 14

G
global warming 28

H
hemisphere 7
hurricane 6, 9, 18, 23

L
landslide 14
lightning 9, 17, 18, 19, 20, 21

M
mesocyclone 19
meteorologist 26, 27
migration 24

P
polar region 28

R
radiation 6
rainwater 13

S
satellite 26, 27

sea levels 28
sniffer dog 23
snow 6, 8, 12, 13,
    22, 23
snowflake 13, 23
snowmobile 23
storm chasers 18
supercells 18

T
thunderstorm 9, 18, 20
tornado 9, 17, 18
torrential rain 18
tsunamis 14, 15

U
updrafts 19

V
vapor 12, 13, 17

W
waves 14, 15
weather map 27
wildlife 29
wind 6, 9, 10, 11, 14, 15,
    18, 19, 22, 27

Websites

Due to the changing nature of Internet links, PowerKids Press has developed an online list of websites related to the subject of this book. This site is updated regularly. Please use this link to access the list:
www.powerkidslinks.com/disc/weath/